WEATHER

SNOW
AND US

Jillian Powell
Illustrated by Cilla Eurich

Smart Apple Media

First published in the UK in 1998 by
Belitha Press Limited
London House, Great Eastern Wharf,
Parkgate Road, London SW11 4NQ

Text by Jillian Powell   Illustrations by Cilla Eurich
Text and illustrations copyright © Belitha Press Ltd 1998
Cover design by The Design Lab

Published in the United States by
Smart Apple Media
123 South Broad Street
Mankato, Minnesota 56001

ISBN: 1-887068-39-2

Library of Congress Cataloging-in-Publication Data
Powell, Jillian.
    Snow and us / Jillian Powell : illustrated by Cilla Eurich.
       p.   cm. — (Weather)
    Includes index.
    Summary: Describes snow and how it is formed, ways people enjoy it, and some of the
problems it can cause.
    ISBN: 1-887068-39-2
    1. Snow—Juvenile literature. 2. Weather—Juvenile literature.
[1. Snow.] I. Eurich, Cilla, ill. II. Title. III. Series: Powell, Jillian. Weather.
QC926.37.P68   1998
551.57'84—dc21   98-11196

Printed in Hong Kong

9   8   7   6   5   4   3   2   1

Picture acknowledgements:
First Light: 28 Jessie Parker.
Getty Images: 8 Michael Buselle, 16 Everett Johnson, 20 Richard Johnson,
22 Kathy Bushue, 24 David Hiser, 26 Chris Noble.
Frank Lane Picture Agency: 6 L. West, 12 Martin Withers, 14 M.J. Thomas.
Spectrum Colour Library: 10 G.R. Richardson, 18.
Stockmarket/Zefa: front cover Kehrer.

Contents

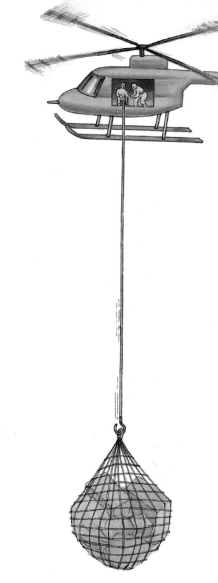

Words in **bold** are explained
on pages 30 and 31.

What is snow?

When did you last see snow? The coldest parts of the world have snow all year round. Most parts of the world have snow only in winter.

SNOW FACT

Every time it snows, millions of snowflakes fall.

In some hot countries it never snows, except on the highest mountains.

Snow is made high up in the clouds. Inside clouds there are billions of droplets of water.

If the air in the cloud is cold enough, the droplets freeze into ice.

As more water freezes on the specks of ice, they grow into tiny snow **crystals**. These stick together to make snowflakes.

If the air stays cold enough, snow starts to form and fall.

Snowflakes

One snowflake can be made from hundreds of ice crystals. It looks like a beautiful star. Every snowflake has six points, and each has its very own design. If you look closely, you'll see that every snowflake is **unique.**

It won't be easy to see the separate snowflakes if you catch them on your hand. They stick together as they fall. Try catching them on a piece of black paper instead.

If the air is very cold and dry, small snowflakes fall and make dry powdery snow.

If the air is only just freezing and wet, much bigger snowflakes fall.

Big wet flakes stick together. This snow makes the best snowballs and snowmen.

How snow changes things

The wind makes snow swirl against walls and hedges, and blows it into deep piles called snowdrifts.

Once snow has settled, it doesn't melt right away. The sun's **rays** bounce off of the surface of the snowdrift.

SNOW FACT

Snow **reflects** the light and makes the ground look bright, even at night.

Snow outlines the shape of everything, making the world look unfamiliar and beautiful. Snow settles on gateposts, railings, and mailboxes. Trees look magical in the snow.

When snow falls, it **muffles** sounds so that everything seems silent and still. Crisp snow crunches underfoot.

Wet snow splashes and makes puddles. This kind of snow is called slush.

Ice and frost

Tiny droplets of water in the air turn into frost when they touch freezing things. Frost makes twigs and branches sparkle in the sunshine, and it makes feathery patterns on glass.

SNOW FACT

1 centimeter of rain freezes into about 10 centimeters of snow.

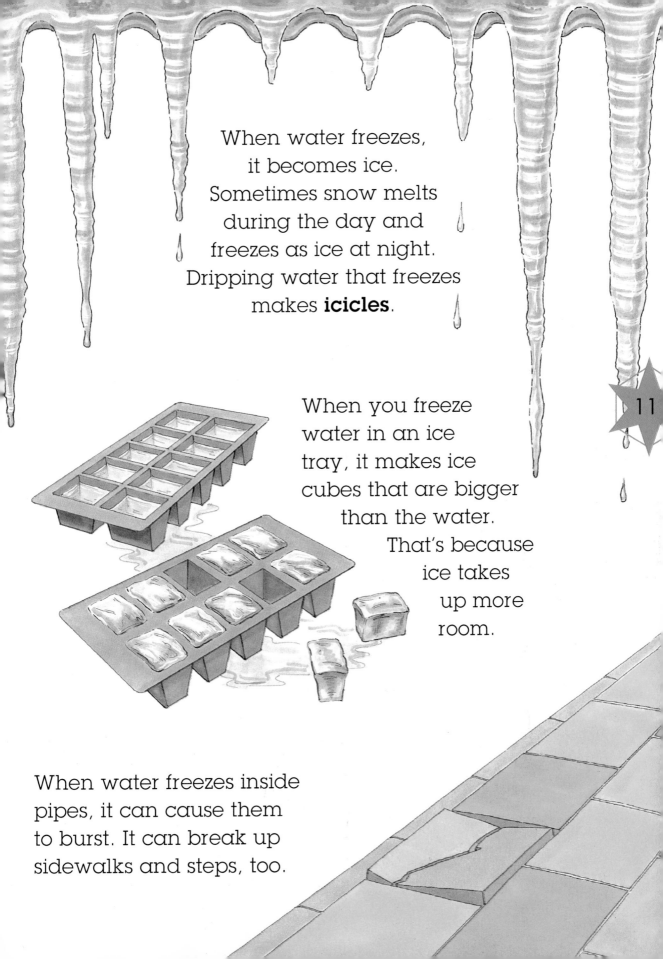

When water freezes,
it becomes ice.
Sometimes snow melts
during the day and
freezes as ice at night.
Dripping water that freezes
makes **icicles**.

When you freeze
water in an ice
tray, it makes ice
cubes that are bigger
than the water.
That's because
ice takes
up more
room.

When water freezes inside
pipes, it can cause them
to burst. It can break up
sidewalks and steps, too.

Snow fun

You can have lots of fun in the snow. You can go for a walk, make a snowman, throw snowballs, or go sledding.

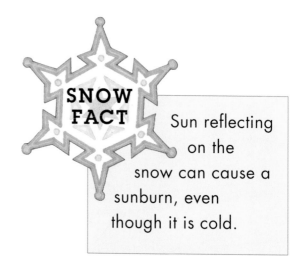

SNOW FACT

Sun reflecting on the snow can cause a sunburn, even though it is cold.

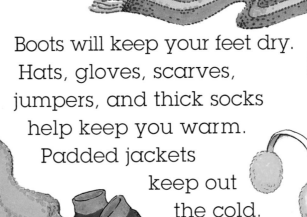

Boots will keep your feet dry.
Hats, gloves, scarves,
jumpers, and thick socks
help keep you warm.
Padded jackets
keep out
the cold.

In places that have lots of snow
in winter, like Canada and the
Northern U.S., people enjoy
snow sports such as skiing
and **snowboarding**. They wear
goggles to protect their eyes
from the bright white snow.

When you come inside
from playing in the
snow, you can warm
up with a hot drink.

Snow problems

A heavy snowfall can block roads. People find it difficult to get to work, and schools may have to close.

Snowplows and **snowblowers** are used to clear the snow. Trucks spread sand or cinders on the roads. This helps tires grip the road so that vehicles don't skid.

SNOW FACT
When snow begins to melt at the end of the winter, it is called a thaw. Water from melting snow can cause flooding.

14

Trucks also spread salt, and people put salt on their doorsteps and driveways when it is snowing.

Salt helps to keep snow from turning into ice because salt water needs to be much colder than fresh water before it can freeze.

Snow can cut off, or isolate whole towns or cities. Sometimes packages of food may have to be dropped from helicopters.

Staying safe in the snow

When the weather is windy and snowy at the same time, a **blizzard** can form. **Weather forecasters** tell people to stay indoors.

SNOW FACT Pond ice freezes unevenly. It is dangerous and can break if you walk on it.

Snow makes it difficult for us to walk outside. In places like Alaska, snow remains almost all year round, and people often **ski** from place to place.

People should drive slowly in snowy weather. Car and bus tires can have snow chains put on them to keep them from skidding.

Sheep can be buried under snow. Farmers have to make sure that their animals are safe and have enough food to eat.

Animals in winter snow

Animals need more food in the winter to make **energy** to keep them warm. But when snow covers the ground, it is hard for wild animals to find food and water.

Putting out food and water for birds can help keep them alive in winter weather.

SNOW FACT

Voles dig tunnels in the snow, because it keeps out icy winds.

Sometimes you may see **tracks** in the snow. These tracks could have been made by cats, deer, dogs, squirrels, or birds.

Some animals make a **nest** and sleep through the winter to escape the cold and snow. This is called **hibernation**.

The coats of some animals, such as ermines, turn from dark to white in winter. This lets them hide easily from **predators**.

Plants and trees in the snow

Pine and fir trees have limber or pliant branches that bend but don't break under heavy snow. Instead of leaves, they have tough, shiny needles that let the snow slide off easily.

SNOW FACT

In the snow-fields of some mountains, tiny plants called lichens make the snow look pink or green.

A sudden frost or snowfall can kill plants that aren't ready for the winter. Some plants **adapt** to cold weather very well.

Holly has a waxy covering on its leaves that traps the heat of the sun and keeps them warm in winter.

Snow buttercups make a little heat to melt the snow while they are growing.

Mosses grow close to the ground for protection from the cold.

Animals in snowy lands

Polar bears live on the arctic shores of Alaska and Canada. They have small noses and ears, so they do not lose too much **body heat** in the air. They grow thick, white fur coats that keep them warm and let them hide in the snow.

SNOW FACT

The coldest, snowiest places on earth are around the North and South Poles.

Snowy owls have thick feathers on their legs and feet to keep out the cold.

Reindeer have wide hoofs that keep them from sinking too deep into the snow.

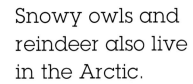

Snowy owls and reindeer also live in the Arctic.

Arctic

Antarctic

Penguins live in **Antarctica**, near the sea. They have thick layers of feathers. Baby penguins keep warm by sitting on their parents' feet.

People in snowy lands

The **Inuit** people live in the snowy lands of Canada and Greenland. They live with snow and ice all year round.

Their traditional clothes were made from animal furs and sealskins.

SNOW FACT

The Inuit have many words for snow. Qanik means dry, powdery snow.

24

In the past, the Inuit lived in snow houses made from blocks of ice. They traveled over the snow on sleds pulled by teams of dogs.

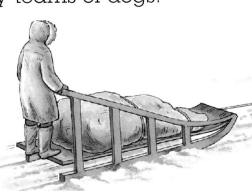

Today, most Inuit live in wooden houses, often built on **stilts** above the snow.

They still use snowhouses for shelter when they are out hunting for meat and fish.

They use **snowmobiles** more often than sleds to ride over the snow.

Mountain snow

The air near the top of tall mountains is very cold. That's because high mountain tops have a cover of snow, even in the summer. The Himalayas near Nepal have snow all year long. In the local language, Himalaya means 'home of snow'.

SNOW FACT

Avalanches can move as fast as 125 miles (200 km) an hour, burying villages and killing people.

Sometimes the snow on a mountain begins to slide downward. This is called an **avalanche**. It makes a rumbling sound like thunder.

Loud noises, melting snow, or skiers may start an avalanche.

Fences help stop snow from moving too far. Trees can also protect villages.

Rescue teams with dogs search for people trapped on snowy mountains. Helicopters carry people to safety.

Snow stories and festivals

In countries where lots of snow falls in the winter, people often hold snow **festivals**. In Canada they carve huge figures from the snow.

SNOW FACT

In **Inuit** stories, *Nootaikok* is the spirit of icebergs. He helps the Inuit find seals.

The Japanese have a
snow festival in February.
Children make snow
houses and sleep in them
all night. They light
candles inside for the
spirits who bring water.

Some people believe
there is a monster called
the yeti that lives in
the snowy Himalaya
mountains. They say that
it leaves giant footprints in
the snow.

Words to remember

adapted To become used to a new place or way of doing something.

Antarctic The name for an area of land and sea around the South Pole. It is covered in thick ice and snow.

Arctic The name for an area of land and sea around the North Pole. It is covered in thick ice and snow for most of the year.

avalanche A mass of snow and ice, earth, or rock that slides very fast down a mountainside or cliff.

blizzard A snowstorm.

body heat Warmth stored in the body.

crystals Flat-sided shapes that are made when a liquid hardens.

energy Energy gives people, plants, and animals strength to do things, or to grow.

festival A time when people celebrate.

goggles Glasses or masks with dark lenses that protect people's eyes from the sun.

grit Rough, hard bits of stone or sand.

hibernation When an animal sleeps through the winter in a safe and warm place.

icicles Pointed sticks of ice made when running or dripping water freezes.

Inuit A group of people who live in the Arctic.

lichen Simple plants that don't have roots, stems, leaves, or seeds.

mosses Small, flat, plants that grow in damp places.

muffle To make a sound quieter.

nest A hollow home of twigs or leaves made by an animal or bird.

predator An animal that hunts and kills other animals for food.

rays Thin lines, or beams, of light and heat.

reflect When sunlight bounces back from a bright surface.

ski To travel on skis.

snowblower A machine that blows the snow off roads.

snowboarding A sport where people glide down snowy slopes standing on a smooth board.

snowmobiles Motor vehicles specially made to travel across snow.

snowplow A machine that pushes snow to the sides of the road.

spirit Something people believe in, but can't see, hear, or touch (for example, a ghost).

stilts Posts that hold a building up above ground or water level.

tracks Animal footprints.

unique One of a kind.

weather forecaster Someone who tells us what the weather will be like.

31

Index